STONES CALL OUT

STONES CALL OUT

PAMELA PORTER

COTEAU
BOOKS

Edited by Elizabeth Philips.
Cover and book design by Duncan Campbell.

Cover image: "Naked Crouching Man" by Mia Klein / Getty Images.

Printed and bound in Canada at Gauvin Press.

Library and Archives Canada Cataloguing in Publication

Porter, Pamela Paige, 1956-
    Stones call out / Pamela Porter.

Poems.
ISBN 1-55050-340-5

I. Title.

PS8581.07573S76 2006   C811'.6   C2006-901214-8

1 2 3 4 5 6 7 8 9 10

COTEAU BOOKS

2517 Victoria Ave.
Regina, Saskatchewan
Canada S4P 0T2

Available in Canada and the US from:
Fitzhenry & Whiteside
195 Allstate Parkway
Markham, Ontario
Canada L3R 4T8

The publisher gratefully acknowledges the financial assistance of the Saskatchewan Arts Board, the Canada Council for the Arts, the Government of Canada through the Book Publishing Industry Development Program (BPIDIP), Association for the Export of Canadian Books, the Government of Saskatchewan, through the Cultural Industries Development Fund, and the City of Regina Arts Commission, for its publishing program.

 Canada Council for the Arts / Conseil des Arts du Canada SASKATCHEWAN ARTS BOARD   Canada Regina CITY OF REGINA Regina Arts Commission

*For Rob, who sees
into the dazzling darkness*

contents

I. A CLOUD OF WITNESSES

II. STONES CALL OUT

III. OPEN GATE

"I tell you, if these were to keep silence, the very stones would cry out."
— Luke 19:40

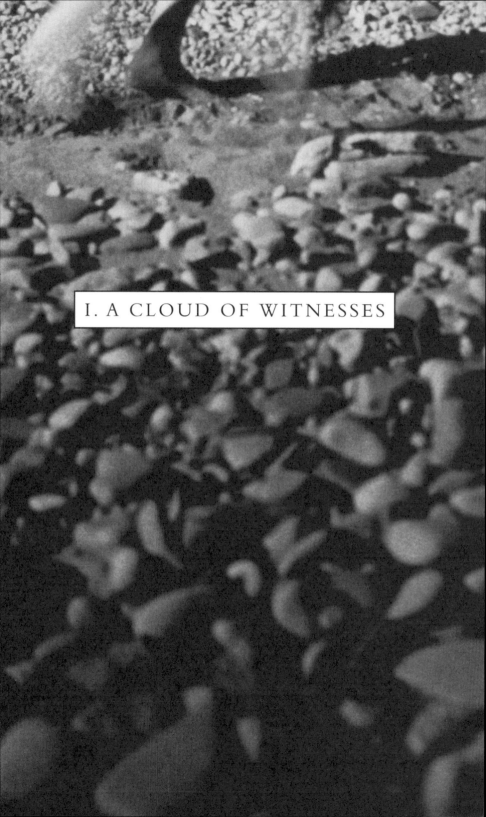

I. A CLOUD OF WITNESSES

BEARERS OF DARKNESS

In 1914, coal miners in Ludlow, Colorado went on strike.
Evicted from their houses, miners and their families were living
in tents when vigilantes and the Colorado Militia moved in,
killing twenty men, women, and children.

1.

Night without moon, night worn
with the last, still-echoing day
begins the dull sliding of wood against wood,
mute figures by one weak lamp
lifting coffin after coffin, cimmerian white.
The burdened wagons quietly groan.
Harness leather creaking, a mule
rolls its blind eyes back, stamps a hoof
into earth stubborn with frost
as a wolf, then wolf mate, float their thin howls
across the blood dark air, ground stained hard with blood.

2.

It was early on the day and dark.
Shadows swelling, no wind. Through a shuttered window,
street light fingered the floor, the bed, the boy
wakened by voices on the porch.
His father. The sheriff. *Round up a gang,*
get you some kerosene, the sheriff ordered.
Light up them strikers' tents till the militia comes.
The boy could feel half-forgotten angers
swelling the streets, the air so heavy with them,
he found breathing difficult. He turned
and the iron bed on which he lay
moaned and murdered the silence.

3.

By afternoon's bleak sun
a caravan of bone snakes into town.
Children who lived, mothers, wives,
miners who lived, have wheeled their dead
all the way from Ludlow and lead their mules
down Trinidad's main road,
under militiamen's sleepy gaze. The boy,
who knew before it happened,
keeps vigil in the vee of a roof. Blaze
of candlelight in church windows.

By dusk, the miners who lived and the children
and women who lived, sift the last cemetery dirt
and load their shovels.
The wagons' hollow clatter wanes.
That is all. Nothing more
but a draft of wind between church doors
and candlelight pulsing
beneath the crucifix, over the baby, a doll
nestled in hay. All night the crucifix
is cast swollen and bent across the ceiling,
and the infant's shadow multiplies, *Agnus Dei,* on the walls.

Before the dark mouths
of the hills mined clean, the old cars
rust deeper into their tracks, heavy
with useless stone. The only tree in town
stands stooped, nearly bare
by the filling station's wall. Oscuro, town
forsaken, hangs by wind's grace:
the church bell worked loose of its rope,
howl of smokestack, cemetery gate.
Where Raúl once lived, migrants –
leaves, tumbleweeds – drift through the door
left open the day he carried chair,
table, his straw mattress
to the mine owner's house, three-storied green,
where a dappled horse still prowls the hills
and searches the barn for scraps of hay.

Behind the porch, shredded lace curtains,
spare front room, Raúl lights the stove,
turns lumps of dough between his palms.
Father Reyero will come grinding up the road
in that stammering auto, and although Raúl
does not believe, there are so few left to visit.
That is the reason Father comes, bringing
flour, cans, and now, news of the child
Raúl only the night before held in his arms.
He'd carried her down the road that wound
to the highway. He'd lied to her in the night:
Tu mamá, Dulcita, está solo dormido –
their only light a reflection of moon
off the adobe church wall and the shabby
cluster of cemetery crosses.

Halfway down the hill loose with sliding
rock, out of the car's shattered window
he'd lifted the child: her mother, Rebecca,
who cooked at the diner in Pastura, lay caught
under metal and the reek of vanilla
he'd once seen her drink. It was the yellow
glare of her headlights that first called him
to his window, grazed the walls of his unlit room.
Even before the crash, the horse fled
from the murmur of her approach
that fractured the windless night.

Noon. Broken sunlight brushes past Oscuro
and travels on. Snow fills the crevasses in rocks
crumbling on their rusted tongue of track. Father Reyero,
on his last visit, one foot poised to descend
the porch steps, his lungs filled with the cold,
said, *When we are crucified, He is also* – and stopped,
remembering Raúl's disbelief – *it is larger
than ourselves, death.*
Ritual rhythms fill the kitchen: a car's
far-off growl, the pat between his palms
of tortilla Raúl watches grow round, bright
like a moon, a soul, a little sun
there among the decaying walls.

In broad, high places where clouds
move shadows down distant cliffs,
the sounds of old years gather.
One learns to lean to hear them, then hearing
is easy: the delicate, white-pink skull of a deer
fallen to its place in the sand; a hawk
floating out of cloud shadow, turning its red tail
to the sun; a lavender flower
rooted in a cedar stump.
Where power lines give out,
I leave the truck, walk the last mile
to the hogan of Luther Kayate.
From this rise I can just make out his house,
corral of ocotillo stalks, sheep like lace
grazing among the valley's stunted brush.

In March I first brought the box of flour,
cheese, beans, butter. He shuffled to the door,
stood bent, hand against the frame,
eyes falling upward as though toward sleep.
I gave my name, told about the box.
He repeated my name as if it were a song,
then asked was I a relative
of the man who once was sheriff of Gallup –
my grandfather's brother.
The year I was born, he shot two Navajo boys
running through the dark down Copper Avenue,
having done nothing
but run through the dark.
"No," I said,
looking at his eyes.

Always,
Luther Kayate comes to the door the same –
bent, hand against the frame
and with alarming accuracy takes the box.
But this day, Luther invites me in.
His dishcloth hangs beside the door
above its enamel basin. On his table,
the clean separation of plate, cup, and spoon.
I hear his feet scrape the floor, see
his hands stir light on his bed
where they lie – the moccasins –
wine-coloured leather, silver buttons reflecting sun.
He holds them out for me.
I test their weight, Luther close to my shoulder
and breathing. I turn them in the light,
all the invisible dead gathered in them, singing.

When, exactly, the silent trespass of rust
first took the roof, or the fire-wheel daisy
the phlox beside the road, is lost from memory.
How long ago the old car's clay tracks
began the intangible giving over to grass
is more than Lizzie can say.
One day the dog appeared on the porch.
Then the mantel clock ran down.
Nights now, near dusk, her husband's wailing –
like a goat or lamb – that bleating
after some ancient claim, estranged,
rises from the house, is borne over town,
but of its beginning or ending
no one in Henderson can say.

The dog flicks an ear, chin on its paws
beside the door, won't leave.
Wednesday nights, rear of the church,
Lizzie leans into the end of the pew, studies
stained light falling through the windows,
and when the offering basket comes round, Hilda
whispers, *Take what you need, Lizbeth...don't be starvin'*
*yourselves...*Nearly dark, the pump organ's whine
trails her down the road, meets his anguished
rising and falling as one sound
seeking the hidden spaces, while Mrs. Rose
closes window after window, nine o'clock
beating through her rooms.

But on the dirt road that curves away from town,
where two-roomed houses lean, scattered along
unusable land, elders
have carried kitchen chairs to the yard.
Often they tilt their heads, consider
the scarred, ochre dirt, witness
the sounds at dusk and the curtain
of night falling on the brief,
red truth of sky.
Then may come a nod,
a low rumble in the throat: assent.

Queene:
Memory moves in like storm
certain days or nights, of that hot April
just before noon, the thought finally seized,
your '65 Buick fell easily, it seemed
toward the Volkswagen coming on,
its windshield clobbered with light.
Buick, violent foot,
crushed metal flat into his unseen
face, your suicide failed.
Hard to think how you arrived from childhood
to this, here, this morning, as the incessant sun
works bright bars onto your bed; to think
after serving nine months you got off,
walked pot-holed roads framed by cane
back to this city smelling of liquor and mould,
where the slow moan of tugboats' horns
wakes you from merciful sleep.

Nearly clean of food, you rise
and powder your alabaster skin, born
of a seamen's gang near Bienville and Clay,
or so your mother said when she meant
to hurt, or wanted your pity. You slide your feet
into something plastic and cheap, start downstairs
past musty lines of mailboxes. Heavy August.
It's too early; the corner market's corner doors
are shut behind their curled screens.
Stopped still on the porch steps, you can't
even think, such a morning as this, when
waking, you half dreamed his face
through the windshield's glare, clear
and young. What the hell have you been
chosen for, had birth thrust upon you,
death lifted from reach?

It's crazy how things keep on,
like this asphalt-painted-over-brick street
that trucks growl their gears past,
and across at the church where you kneeled
until you were seventeen, doors wide open
as a mouth, workmen hoist new pillars
under the roof. Even here
you can feel the ground shake.

Then around a corner a tune comes
as every morning at quarter to nine,
the clarinet player almost dancing toward the square,
hat torn, hair bushed out, the instrument
nearly swallowed in his beard.
This time, you call out: *That's mighty good.*
Then, music stopped, to fill the silence:
You eaten?
Lady, I ain't eaten for two days.
Sit here. As you ascend the steps
the music rises from the porch,
bends, straightens, bends again, and for once,
it comes out right in the end.

Sunrise. Such silence
she'd never heard in her fourteen years.
All her life the coal cars switched, shrieked
without pause for the unrestrainable dark.
That monstrous fan leached its life
from the valley of gaunt pines.
Now on the mountain it peers, battered bird,
over the village covered in a ration of grief:
soot-dusted rows of sagging roofs,
dishcloths stiffened and black
on their lines, the geranium, black.
Jesse's arm black from its swipe across the windshield.
Sky sapphire, itinerant clouds grow frail gold.

She couldn't sleep, so dressed and wandered
through the devastated town, and now dawn,
finds herself in the driver's seat of the car
she's too young to drive. Her hand
rakes her red hair, elbow in the window frame,
can't stop her brain repeating
that sudden seizure of earth, sound
of their china tumbling down the shelf as smoke
and blue flame rushed the mouth of the mine.
The sound of everything breaking.
The dog, dreaming, fidgets, then yelps. In the house
her mother must at last be sleeping.
It is summer.

She heard his voice last evening in the store —
There I was, last one out before the fire —
and dared a glance into her father's orange beard
permanent with dirt. Always it was
as if he'd never seen her, never
had those years with her mother.
Wrapped in Johnnie's Ford, she tried to form
dark-haired Johnnie from the dawn,
would will him out of the mine to fill
his trousers on her mother's chair, to unwrap his watch
claiming time on her mother's bedpost,
to rest his hand on Jesse's neck
as they walked to the store for ice cream,
the hills of coal blazing violet in paling light.

But it is a Tuesday,
the future quickly ripening:
by noon her father will pass by, red beard
waving, in the back of a westbound truck. At dusk
they'll find Johnnie in some miles-deep room
effluent with gas, above him the inscription:

> *Walter and Johnnie. Goodbye*
> *wives and daughters. We died*
> *an easy death. Be good.*

Some grief ancient to her own
will brood in her and swell
the shrouded town. All
the moonstruck, splintered houses
will hear it
calling itself
to itself.

Owl, see my squinted surprise – it's sudden
recognition. Light flaming horizontal
around you, you've eclipsed the sun again,
that flat head of yours pointed earthward,
neither questioning this daylight stance nor me
aching to peer inside your silhouette
for the judicial beak, oracular eyes I remember.

How could I forget? You were odd that way even then,
arbiter on some branch in the yard by afternoon,
different pine, colder spring – that bad Wednesday
I never forgave you for. As I beat my skates
against my leg home, daily guessing
your position, you'd already spotted me.
Head side, front, imperially sure.

Nights I'd breathe into my blankets
and strain the quiet for your call,
rustle, rush, then gone beyond sleep.
You always came back.
That day Grandpa died,
I waved Mother out the driveway
toward the funeral in Medicine Hat

and, ward of Mrs. Flowers,
I searched all your quirky perches. That night,
for thump or whirl – some sign of you,
I waited out the dark, silence buzzing my ears
until their voices pressed in: Grandpa,
that last summer morning, stroking my hair,
promising he'd visit; Mother's voice

low and faltering as I turned my back:
A funeral's no place for children. How Mr. Jensen
from next door – the one whose wife left, taking the children
and that dog you pestered – sat beside me
on our steps and spoke of you. He'd seen us,
and pointed to the empty branch where sun
sailed into our eyes. Owl,

I never tried to keep you;
you were free to come and go.
That Saturday when Grandpa was buried
in a wet, grey snow, I vowed to forget you,
baked Grandma's chocolate cake
careful stroke by stroke, and with Mrs. Flowers asleep,
wrapped and placed it at Mr. Jensen's door,

then walked my longest path home
past the brush-jammed, brown stream
and early dogwood in bloom. It was your cry
I heard – made me stop sudden, peer
into the dense pines – you were hidden.
I turned toward the house, climbed the steps,
and opening the door full,

I walked into that darkness on my own.

THE LETTERS

After WWI some soldiers exposed to mustard gas
were sent to Arizona either to recover or slowly die.

Before the oak wardrobe, I breathe
the odour of ages. Ruth
has sent me to find her gold
leaf brooch.

My hand
in a shadowed corner
brushes a small bundle: eight letters
tied with string, mildewed
and brittle, four from France,
four from Arizona.

The letters have lain as long
as her laundry basket
against the back door.
They began to arrive here
before she pulled his coat
down from its nail

on the frame of the unfinished house
whose ghost still creaks
on that unsectioned scrap of prairie
not half a mile away.

If I turn slowly, I might glimpse
Ruth's tattered dress, limp
over the chair, the patched
cotton-sack slumped onto the floor.
They will be everywhere they have been,

waiting for him, for his letters. Daily
she dragged the sack
into the fields, sliced
her hands on the sharded bolls
guarding the smoke-white center.

Ruth's hands, bent
and arthritic, rest on the arms
of the chair where she waits
for her gold leaf brooch.

And one corner
of an envelope crumbles
like his shattered lungs
in my hand.

In memory of Ruth Parker
— 1903-1993

VIGIL

After forty-five years that Friday still lives
in memory – the wrenching of his sudden
leaving, and the unveiling to my sight
of the inextricable web of things, dependencies:
for its life that bruised evening
needed a rain-soaked morning, the particular autumn
snow in spring, his exodus
his bloody birth. A poor crop snapped
what long had smoldered under his roof,
and I, eighteen, already had burned his face,
his nineteen-year-old neighbour hands
into my memory. I want even now to tell him
his father's jaw did not break.
By the sole light
of apple wood I watched from my ladder, veiled by branches
while hills blackened into the sky
and young trees sprouting from the water tower
lost their form to darkness.

That night along my dirt-lined palms
I traced his tracks, his train that lurched
over the trestle we'd so delicately walked.
I pictured towns surrendered to wilderness:
fruit crates stacked in empty lots, blurred
in passing; another's laundry slouched
beside its stiffened house.
On the hills, aspens
had no choice but to be transformed
by darkness, but I – face,
hands bereft of colour – I searched
his window, while through my lace
curtain, some light, its source hidden,
emerged, withdrew behind a fissured cloud.

In time I would hear though not yet see
the finch rustle in its nest, and at last
perceive what unearthly passion
had gathered us to itself,
rushed into that night with our unravelling, as fruit
of gnarled trees hung reddening
and frail birds waited, breathless. At dawn
I lay and watched the clear sky
brighten, the hills grow rust,
gold, unable to close my eyes
to such passion rising beyond the glass, the same
that once caught us up,
from which, after forty-five years, I cannot turn my face,
and even now bear the stone of its weight.

My half-eaten tortilla she placed over her son's
bowl of beans. When tortillas were not enough
her breasts withered dry. Daily
her husband stood in line for work.
The baby sucked nonetheless.
I know this.
Late I sat under her light bulb
beside the cooking fire while others
across Chimaltenango slept, some
whispered in the dark. As my belly
bulged with sleep her husband
told their story.
It is a good day he doesn't come home
until dark, was all she said. Maria,

you must know my house
is covered in carpet. Even
the kitchen. Nights when my baby
stirs and cries I call on the angel of sleep
and when the angel herself sleeps,
I raise myself and go.
My daughter has a room as big as your shack.
My breasts ache with milk.
I won't tell you how many bathrooms. Tonight
the grasses sleep beneath the same moon,
but we don't need to farm.
I've heard about the strike, that workers
have died. In the dark I form his face
at your door each night, hear
your neighbours tell under their hats how God
has chosen the poorest of the poor
to carry Christ's cross, rebuild the ruined
cities of the rich.

Tomorrow perhaps, I'll buy myself a hat.
Something to do.
I am tired with my life,
terrified of yours.

AWAKENING

Bleached white, in an even line across the windowsill,
the little shells, each broken or worn to its core,
lie obedient to the pass light makes
through them. Already the scent
of roses lifts her from sleep, from some dream
of a face familiar as her breath, that vanishes
with her first blink. Still
on the nightstand the palmetto-leaf cross,
the memory slow returning: how yesterday
she twirled it between her fingers in the crowded pew,
and seeing the stranger with receding hair
watching her, drew her eyes to the open window
where bees droned and gulls, distant,
called each other across the sky.

Blonde hair side parted, wire glasses
burdening her nose, she slips out the picket
gate and down the white road, searching endless marsh
for the sea, always beyond sight. In her hand
the biscuit Mrs. Wheeler who boarded her
had placed there. Her skin had shivered
where those hands, without rage, grasped hers.
Knobby, liver-spotted as her mother's ferocity-crazed
hands, they yet had admired her hair, their delicate
touch to her head nearly frightening.
Still seventeen, the memory of family
blurred faceless by day,
but cleared in violet dreams
between the last, moth-battered lamplight
and the pure clang of the school bell.

A gravid quiet. Heat
dampens her dress.
Past marsh grass beaten limp,
her feet press shells into the road as she thinks
of last night's storm, the lighthouse beam
warping through their street, how all muffled
day something seemed to whisper
her name: *Katie, Kate.*
Thunderheads gathering,
across the dingy church she eyed
the stranger, his suit fine, shoes shined,
an unspeakably gentle face that turned
to hers. Above, a moth buffeted the lamp.
What? What is it? Call and question.
Rain began.

This good Monday, stain of wine
still on her tongue, along store fronts
ordinary labours appear liquid as light,
translucent against the transparent
sky. In the kitchen, assurances are waiting:
the crack-infested teapot,
cookies on a yellow plate.
Not far, the stranger stops walking, startled,
his glasses gleaming suns. She fingers the latch.
The schoolyard gate's rusted hinges
sing. Near her hair a bee
nuzzles its luminous self in the tangle
of trellis, intimate among the battered roses.

In memory of Kate Parker
— *1897-1992*

II. STONES CALL OUT

BENEDICTION

Rosa, Rosa Salazar,
how did you hear it then,
in those years when God was absent?
You whom I knew as myself
would toss your meager frame
from the school bus door, and linger
as it gnashed its yellow weight and turned,
a lumbering tortoise, in the road. At the edge of Fate,
Texas, with your lethargic shoes, it is over,
the last day of ninth grade, and you wander
toward Mrs. Macalester's roses, wishing
she'd appear from behind the house, perspiring
in her hat and calico gloves, the only white woman
who speaks to you. On windy bus rides through early cotton
you've imagined that she is your mother
and brushes your black hair each night beside your bed,
and teaches you complex prayers
God will hear. Rosa, it is a tiny miracle
she bends over the porch rails and asks you in.

At her table you sip her minty, sugared tea and try
to conceive how you'll stay until Mother gets home,
then weather Frank's muzzled anger; of a summer
of mornings when he'll slide from under the car
and take his fingers to the button on your shorts,
his hand a vise at your waist.
After he's closed your door
and the screen has quaked you'll lie
in the spiraling silence of God's absence
until the grass beside the tracks
behind your house begins singing
the lullaby never far buried in your brain
that your father sang those weeks in bed,

and you, nearly seven, lay
your head on his abscessed chest, felt
his heart's clumsy beat. Rosa,
Mrs. Macalester fills your glass, makes
a guess after your summer. I know what moves
behind your unplucked brows: you half envy
those girls dressed to kill and speeding in some boy's
car toward Dairy Queen and the lake.
You shrink at the cost you think they pay.

That sultry sky turned greenish,
she sends you home at first thunder. Too soon.
Hammered by wind, the bowing roses are singing
as he sang that day the ambulance came
quietly, compounding the quiet, the day
he disclosed how he'd sung to you
in the womb, and after, how, hearing,
you let out a cry and turned
at last to see him.
Even in hell, Rosa, we still could hear it
as rose, grass, the very stones
calling their pledge, our benediction.

HOW THE MIRACULOUS
CAME SO CLOSE TO ULM, MONTANA

The morning they came, and found him, and took
him away, they came in uniforms in the sooty
still-dark when one may (if one is awake and waiting
for something, a sign from God) despair of dawn
returning. The yellowed lights of their sedan
dipped, curved onto the road, the official seal
spattered with mud under the chants of elm
and oak, beside the prayers of grass.
In its nest above the river, the eaglet crouched,
closed-eyed beside its mother. Across the prairie,
mountains yet invisible lifted their daily office.

They found him in the pump house
into which he'd wandered after straying
through the mental hospital gates. Lizzie
had heard his calling that May morning
but thought him an animal, trapped,
pump house door ajar, then glimpsed his face,
waxen from years without sun.
She brought him food on a movie house plate,
sent him to gather eggs. Three days
he tossed feed in extravagance, ripped
the strings on all the feed sacks
and herded the chickens while lilacs hung
heavy as censers, and breezes
swung their frail incense into the air.

They took him away in the calm after a night storm.
Perhaps her sister had seen him the day
she stayed to organize the kitchen drawers,
refold the dishtowels. Already, faint colour
pooled in the yard. Lizzie
shook her head at questions
arched from their knotty faces.
He walked with more grace than usual
that moment, his pink hands cuffed
behind him, hair freely on end.
As the Hudson jerked on ruts in the road,
the young eagle tested the air casually, after its mother,
eyeing the river, the expanse of grass,
and letting air take them, rose over the pumphouse,
over the chickens, rose like a sign
(if one is waiting for a sign)
over the world's and Lizzie's
brief transfiguration.

CANYON

In a '62 Plymouth we drove
to the Grand Canyon – Father, Mother
and we two girls – across the desert,
summer, damp towels beating the open
windows, ice between us in a bag.

The day I began my vigil
on our garage floor, 105 degrees,
knees tight to my chest
between the thrown-out dresser
and the tossed couch,
I wanted only for someone to ask,
and perhaps, touch
though I could grasp no words
to describe this chimera.
Mother, Father, then sister looked,
declared, *You'll get heat stroke,*
and finally, annoyed, ignored
while the man who did it
called my name
from the next yard.

Waiting them out, passing
the long hours, I thought
how I had stood at the canyon's edge,
no longer the greatest precipice
I knew. I saw myself in my pink
sandals calling, calling my name
and waiting for an answer
from the blood-coloured walls,
the distant, indifferent water.

MONTANA, EARLY SPRING

200 Minuteman nuclear missiles are stored
in concrete silos in Montana, 150 in North Dakota.

Cecilia
your eyes, when open wide as the blue sky,
predict judgement. At this moment
they're shut behind your fringed lids,
and with pacifier resting upon your chest,
you sleep, another exhausted tourist.
Those mares that all your life
hung their weighty faces over barbed wire
and collected snow on their backs
today gallop thunderous
across the prairie grasses.
The sleeping brush flares red.
My precious, how will I explain
how the earth is planted here in death –
missiles swallowed in concrete,
named for the benignity of time, aimed
at the sky? If I fail
you'll ask, little foal, the suns
of your eyes flaring.
Some days along this thin road
we see one raised up and pointing,
odd obelisk of the plain
among the furtive antelope,
migrating geese.

One day, maybe we'll leave this place
if we can find a more peaceful spot on earth.
With horses, yes, and geese like these
who return every spring, find
the river ready, ice sloughed off.
Like them, something within us
calls us to make a home and hope
for peace enough.

Nine you were when it first whispered
to you: that day so still, not even wind blew
across Saskatchewan,
neighbours carried your grandfather's quilt-wrapped
body down the narrow stairs,
and in the house, alone, you heard
the ticking from his room grow clearer,
distinct. Below your window Grandma
stood German-tall as the car
grumbled to a speck between fields
of wheat stubble and patches of old snow.
You said once you walked that night
down the road toward town, the watch
muffled in your pocket, and when
the Soo Line's dirt-caked headlight
curved east, you didn't wait for the engineer
who'd known him forty years. At two-thirty,
so loud it echoed against the bed,
you padded the groaning hall floor you hated walking
at night and put it back, afraid.

You have not told that story again. Perhaps
you spoke too soon, not the same
as telling that Grandma blamed everyone
for months after his death,
that the vegetables froze in the garden
and even Mother left them to waste.
In front of the stove, you'd squat
mornings, in a blanket, blowing coals,
listening for the train to Shaunavon.
Grandfather would have been up
sliding the watch from his pocket,
a little sun in his stern palm: six o'clock.
You wiped your breath at the ice-edged window
where a headlight glowed in blowing snow.

It was all you took when Grandma
boarded up the house and moved to town.
Yours then, cracked crystal,
brittle leather strap, in silence now
it calls us out of our lives
into the dark places within us
we seldom dare to speak of. In quiet,
the watch comes humming. You lean, listening:
there's a familiar word, an old sound.

— for Rob

Saskatchewan. The evangelist wind
raised snow, whipped it as a conductor
would do, arms and baton pumping air, each
instrument, for sound. The percussion windows
thrummed. And a piano began.

The long-play record popped and cracked.
Miss Bauermann had brought it to class, grade six.
School phonograph, plastic handle,
cardboard case. Holding the disc
between her palms, gingerly, so not to touch

its ebony gleam, Miss Bauermann, perpendicular
to the plain that marked us from birth, who
towered like a mountain, snow on her peak
that didn't melt, said, "Class." And we
faced front. "Mr. Glenn Gould is a pianist."

A miniature baton, the little needle
drew out his star-white sound. Melodies
started again each gated measure. I was ten,
sitting on my chapped hands. A train a mile long
jerked over the sutured land while I rose

toward the atmosphere of that height,
the constellation where Miss Bauermann lived
perpendicular to the plain. That evening
I ate my dinner at our farmhouse table,
my father's cap like a son beside his usual plate.

But I would be, thereafter, a measure out of place.

She stands in the sun-filled room
of the big log house, my daughter at three,
radiant coincidence of DNA: silken curls,
blue eyes. I am there too,
wondering what I can eat to salve
such hunger. Her questions arc across the air
elegant as a double helix and as insistent:
What does the baby look like?
I break open the book, Lennart Nilsson's
masterwork, *A Child is Born*. Cecilia's flat
on her belly in front of the full-colour
pages, feet waving like flags
signaling an important event,
and she sees not her new brother, but herself
as though in a family photograph –
*That's me swimming; there's the face
I had before,* caught by the camera
in an unintended instant –
eyes closed, fists clenched
like little stone tools.

THE VOICE LESSON

My son has carried his boy soprano
into a room with grand piano,
unbalanced towers of sheet music
and attractive soprano teacher. I strain

to hear them above the daily shuffling
of students in the hallway, over the sudden
opening of doors as operatic voices spill out
on wave of piano, a kind of musical surfing.

My son's voice is weightless as cirrus
in a spring sky, guileless as breeze
through the windows of his grade four
classroom. I nearly catch the sound of his voice

when a door opens, and a tenor bellowing
La Donna E Mobile splashes over me,
and all the pianos from opened doors
flood into a cacophony of praise. There –

his teacher is leading him through the scale, singing
A spider's crawling up my leg and again
raised a half-step until, like ascending
a ladder, stretching the limits of his range,

she brings him down, black note
by white note, careful not to let him stumble
so high on the scale; and I remember
how at age nine I sang, unaware

of the purity of my sound until one day
the sun rose with its white light
and I began to think about singing,
about the way I appeared to others.

I sang in front of the bathroom mirror
and it was lost, that innocence
which I can never recover. Yet
this afternoon in the car home,

if I turn off the radio, the rhythmic obligato
of the road will propel him into singing,
not for me, not even for himself,
but for joy —

that crystal which defracts light
into multitudes of colour,
and folds each back, fan-like, one sound
folding, and again unfolding. Joy.

ALAMOGORDO: ON THE FORTIETH
ANNIVERSARY BOMB SITE TOUR

It is a landscape for monasteries, mysteries,
the sting of nearly airless light, mountains
ringing the desert basin brilliant
as mirage and as believable.
To the north lie ebony fields of rock
the earth births, northeast, art-on-stone –
first evidence the universe had begun
to think about itself. Here
in the famous, desolate place, the few of us
who wished to stand in the original crater
received a motorcade escort fit
for royals and criminals.
Checking of vehicles. Helicopter assist.

Arrived at the spot, Oppenheimer's outpost wanes,
moon-coloured. No crater in sight – filled in
years before, they tell us. Ten minutes we have
until the green-clad officers herd us
to our cars, but not before my eye
sees cracklings of the crater
in the way the earth has of shuffling things,
bringing bits to the surface – sand
fused green; dark, transluscent glass.

We snake out as we came, yet numb
and dazed by distance and sun,
each passing ocotillo
seems a many-armed monk
raising his prickly sleeves, his dozen
flowering hands in all directions upward,
as if to point, point: there
swirls the vast, *alleluia,*
incomprehensible universe

which homo sapiens,
walking upright, *kyrie eleison,*
has learned to echo –
great green bang, *dona*
fission, fusion, *nobis*
beginning, *pacem*
and end.

THE PRODIGAL

I.

It returned, the memory, as it was wont to,
that day in warm October, with the rhythmic
chopping of onions, as the birdbath in the back yard
waited for birds, waited in front of the trellis
pealing with roses: *chaos of chickens across*
the dirt floor, Mother down, Father kicking her,
and Ruth, thirteen, chopping onions or potatoes
or what have you, lifted the fragrant knife,
and moving near his back, heard
her rasp, "Don't Ruth — for your sake...."
That was the end of it. It was the year he left.

Who could have told her today would be the one day, scent
of onion on her palms, her sister in bed with that
pathetic heart, that the reddened figure in bow tie and suspenders
pulling itself toward the door by railing and cane
after forty-two years would form itself
as himself? The search for one's necessity
is a worn cane leading backwards.
A squirrel hung head down,
as one will from a birdfeeder,
and a circle of violet iris budded
and bloomed as it needed to on the lawn
behind the white-shirted man, fist head high at the door.

II.

*If he tries to touch you, Ruth — even tries...*Kate
cautioned from bed. He sipped sweet tea
on the porch, the cane leaning, close.
They ate stew and long pauses.
She made up the couch. Into the peace
of darkness he'd brought it all with him: the endless
towns he moved them to, the Model T
he traded Elsie and Howard for — no horses
ever better. Before the grace of glasses
Howard's eyes saw her way to school. He grazed
while she drew outsized numbers on her slate,
and carrying her home, he stopped for passing trains. At ten,
lenses thick as jam jars before her eyes, daily
she and Kate walked the length of the bed
reading newsprint pasted to the wall. *Two girls*
not worth a goddamn, their father would say aloud. God
would damn them. God would damn him
because of them, their mother
shuffling through rooms, bent and quiet.

III.

She considered strangling him with her arthritic hands.
The cane was painful to look on.
In the shade of the porch he'd stare across the lawn.
How come you plant flowers, got no future
to 'em...you always tried to be odd
but you too much like me...always knew
you'd grow up and do the same
as me, and you did...you don't want nobody
to care about you, you never
wanted me to care about you...you girls was always
talking about going to France, now if that wadn't a goddamn
stupid idea, I told you
you'd never get there. Fill me that bucket I'm
gonna wash your windows....
She went in to bathe Kate, hold the glass
of water to her mouth, help her eat.
When the young priest arrived
as usual on Thursday, bringing the elements
in a black box, spreading them out to say Mass
in Latin, as Kate wished, the old man
scraped a ladder across the window
and hung the cane on a rung.
Miserere.
This, thought Ruth, is it − is all of it.
Miserere nobis.
Through the half-obstructed window the birdbath
sat like a chalice on the green lawn, a wren
perched and drinking at its edge.

He's the child we take to the psychiatrist, neurologist, psychologist,
the one who's memorized the map, suggests the route.
We wait in rooms tiresome as dim lamps
for something he can carry into this life.
How far can a stone drop, plumb the bottom of a mind?

That day at the canyon, a hawk skimmed the far cliffs.
Snow fell and clouds swam the sky like whales.
Below us lay the river at a distance deeper than we could fathom.
The path we'd taken rushed ahead into air
and he clung, terrified, to the cliff face.
In the end, I had to go on without him.
Trail obscured by snow, my mule swung its head into the sky
at each switchback, my feet stone with the cold.

In his absence no one could map the tangled route
or say the name for every layer of rock,
could tell how many zeros to their ages, each one
a stone he can taste, ancient as earth in the mouth.

Beneath the line of snow, the trail lay frozen in ice.
My mule's hooves danced like a broken compass,
the way his brain tricks him into alarm.

I came back with news: I've crossed the river.
It slices the earth like a cake.
I rode a bridge anchored into rock. I said, *Achievement,*
the human brain. Something he'd study and rebuild back home.

Our covenant says, I'll go on ahead. Say
it's a winter storm – I'll light rooms struck sudden
with night until he can go there alone. Then
he'll have the labyrinth of his brain,
maps we've etched on stone.

III. OPEN GATE

A MEDICINE FOR THE LIVING

for Hermelinda

In your fifth year
you drowned in your own fluid; lungs
sputtered, rattled the bars
of your chest, tin roof
of your house. The mountains of Guatemala
gagged on January fog. Lovely,
yet more than lovely was your name,
the name birthed by the tongue of your mamá
who rose each morning from her edge
of the bed, felt for the spigot
she guarded like grain, rose
and drew the morning's water.

At the pila, stone cold as a statue in the yard,
she splashed *agua fría* over your head,
combed your hair until it shone,
scrubbed you down to your permanently
ochred feet. Rose of winter,
mucus and blood sudden as words
in your mouth,
string tied about your throat
didn't help, beans scattered in the bed
didn't help, neither
cold coffee for fever nor the Canadian
doctor's liquid, thick as fire,
weighting the shelf, caught in the throat
of its bottle.

And your papá, barely grown himself,
held his head heavy as a hoe
under his hat, refused the social worker
who pleaded for hospital, where
the living, dressed white as ghosts,
roam in and out of rooms. Anita del Valle
who was there once and lived to tell
of it, says *knives, needles.*

Roosters could not cry the fog
apart. Dogs could not.

In the smudged air of the medicaster's house,
in chanting for cry of the Quetzal,
none came and you rose, light
out of your thin blouse, out
of feet and fog and smoke. What
we have left of you, the last
letter from your father
arriving after word of your death,
is this paper kite with paper string
delicate as spirit in the hand
and glinting as if grasped by the insouciant sky
to float over the sad, locked world.

MARE, DYING

That unnameable gate, swift, well-oiled,
loosens its barbed-wire latch.

Each ear of the mare swivels
in a different direction, one

toward the huddled nest of finch
in last summer's weeds, matted as mane,

the other into dream. She listens
for bells hanging limp on the gate.

Muzzle to marbled earth, blind eye up,
good eye down, she won't see

the twin chestnut geldings turn
their white-blazed faces toward the gate.

How casually they stamp the frosted ground.
How daily are the gifts of death.

THE LOCKED HOUSE

Snow flurries.
I stand at the only road in sight,
beside broken post and barbed wire, and look
to the thin meeting of prairie and sky,
beyond the lake, deep silent centre
under the black cut of bare trees.
I feel the grey on sod, grey
against grey sky of the house
behind me, and each succeeds the other
in silence, in holding the years
shut away with the quiet closing of the screen door
that day Mother left them, left Manitoba.

No one is home today.
The carriage house leans into itself;
an elderberry's branches finger the roof.
Mother kept few photographs, never spoke
of what disturbance lies in these rooms,
though from childhood I felt it
and feel it now. I imagine a black Ford
rumbling toward the house, Grandfather's glasses shining back
the round world. I place Grandmother on the porch
and Mother inside leaning, arms folded, at the window.
Perhaps it is that day, lines strung finally out of town,
Grandmother called her from the basement stairs,
and clambering up, my child mother grasped the receiver
and shouted through the sky's grip
into the whole dome of the world.
It was the day the world called.

I think how the prairie must have rung
with her mother's voice, then
her father's: *We know you, you'll fall
apart out there, come cryin' back to us.…*
But there is nothing here to explain
her rage, her tongue, the distant place
her eyes go in anger, nothing
to explain the threat
repeated through generations.

Clear morning after a storm, snow riding the air,
I see her here, in front of the locked house,
her coat flapping in wind. Grandfather,
claiming she'll be back, starts the Ford
and they circle, lurch across the yard.
Turn toward the porch, Mother. I, mark of your future,
stand tangled with the past you gave me,
the one I never knew.

THE TEST

You were nine,
the pain of your shattered elbow
faded, years still to go
before you'd snap your leg
in two places, when you argued
like a lawyer to ride
our trickster gelding, and I,
relenting, lifted you to his back,
your spindle legs dangling
above the stirrups when he
tucked his flanks and bolted,
catapulting mud and grass
into the air while you clutched
the saddle for your life,
growing more breakable
the faster he bore you
through the trees, and sprinting
after, expecting to find you
crumpled to the ground,
I wheeled around
the corner, spotted him
beside the barn, then
you — straight
on his back as though
he were the whole
spinning, heaving world
that had thrown you this
test of holding on
and both of you breathless
and satisfied
that you had passed.

MAP READING

My son lies flat on the carpet
this September afternoon,
the waddling school bus
long passed by. He reads maps,
books of them the way a boy
will read a comic book – legs
spread wide across the floor, chin
dug into one closed fist.

I think: he will know his way
in this life.

In the kitchen I heat oil, garlic,
grind pepper, slice lemon,
remember another autumn
when he was a baby. A bird,
flown down the pipe, trapped
inside the wood stove, beat its wings
as I banged my hands, blackening
with soot, against the stove's walls, frantic
to catch and free a bird that suddenly
was more than bird.

Who knew my son would be
both box and open door
to me, his broad, boy finger
pointing to the map, the particular
road on the page, yellow
as his glinting hair, this bright
afternoon, as the crackling garlic
golden in the pan?

SANTA ELENA CROSSING

Rio Grande River

Señor Luna, the language has failed me.
I cannot tell you that you carried me those mornings
to the front of your leaky rowboat,
my seven-year-old hands clinging to your shirt.
When we'd appear in the shade of these cliffs
you'd call to my father, *Hey, Pintor!*
Then, rich as rocks, your laugh
as you'd set me in the boat and pull us over
the border, rope in your fist,
water mark on your trousers.

The portraits he sketched of your children
(you bribed them with *dulces* to sit)
still must lie in your house
from the day your wife placed them
between the folds of a blanket.
On our way to see crazy Jesús she stopped us,
warned us Jesús was evil, stole goats at night,
hung the skulls in his house. Daily
he rocked in the shade of an ocotillo
and spat in the sand.
She never spoke to us again.

Sometimes we brought oranges.
Now I bring news I cannot say
to you, that my father, *El Pintor*,
has not painted in years. You don't say
that in Santa Elena crazy Jesús is dead,
burned out of his house so long ago
wind has worn clean
the soot about his door.
And you, Gilberto Luna,
pulling me in your rowboat, don't know
that I have come back
to see the places my father painted,
to ride in your leaky boat.
But once he painted you from memory,
bent over this boat in your broad hat,
bailing water with a rusted can, the wind
lifting the tails of your yellow shirt.

ROSITA

Rosita, I am back to search for you
on the road from Española to Truchas,
where I stained my child hands
the colour of earth and blood.

Here you remain, peeking out
from a cracked windowpane,
caught at the edge of my sight.
Grass rustles dry as a snake;
the fence slumps. Chickens
tap the ground like a drum.

Rosita, *flor de mi queres*,
you are the gate
rattled by the bony wind;
you are the leaf
clinging to the ink-scratched oak.
Nimble little flame, you fire
the walls of your adobe
and the Santos dance.

It will be *La Noche Buena*
and you the child I was,
rocking in the truck
between your Abuela tucked in her rebozo
and your Abuelo under his hat
toward the Sanctuario, lit

with a thousand little flames, where
the priest plants a moon, *ojo de Diós,*
on your tongue
and your eyes
the colour of shadows, shine.

I will look for you in all the shadows,
beneath the mountain, a fleshy
grandmother, in rustle of grass,
under the moon.

You are the moon, *ojo de Diós,*
and the *horno* round as moon;
you the bread rising, a dozen
suns, smoke of the pinyon.
Far into the night,
the Santos dance.

That shuttered presence rises so strong this time
you can almost name it, watching him
lay one hand on the truck, his eyes focused far past,
familiar as his straight back, hat tilted
off his forehead, the boyish side part of hair
boxed black-and-gray in one lazy *click*. 1936.
Last week he lost his job. Still, your father
gave in to the travelling photographer
whose hat was more worn than his, whose son
wore a dirtier shirt than yours.
Your sisters, who knew secrets,
would say to you afternoons
over the quiet pouring of ice water: *Charles Roy,*
it's not the same these days –
you don't remember your mother....
Hard as you try to focus it, memory
is only a faint clatter of kitchen dishes,
Mother the scrape of her rose against the screen.

You pass grain bins that weave and glare in the heat,
posters peeling from boarded windows in Clarkton, Malden,
drive onto that sputtering ferry that barely
coughs you up at Memphis. Your father
tells stories you've memorized, but leaves rivers
between them your memory can't fill.
At a boarding house near the depot,
you wake to find him gone, delivering mail
in a plane you never knew he could fly,
and you don't tell him how, each night
as you lie on top of the sheets watching
his shadow on the walk pass the saloon door
he won't enter, clusters of men
hanging on the L&N freight cars
rock by so close, you recall
all night that smell of damp shirts.
Father, this is the way the present
becomes the unspoken past:
at thirteen, you vow you'll leave,
plot the years and wait.
His brush against the doorway
and muffled tick of his watch opens your eyes
and in sepia slant of moonlight
you search the cracked mirror for the man
whose life you don't know or understand.

PERPETUITY

The window glass gives back your waved face;
the pear tree hangs heavy with old fruit.
In this cold dusk
familiar grays are clear:
the house unpainted, the road never paved.
The iron doorknob sits loose and the door
cannot lock. Over years her broad, lined face
has burrowed and changed in your memory,
the flannel feel of her dresses,
the lightness of her step in boots:
the first woman you truly loved.
And now, no longer twelve, you nudge
the door back so the sky,
not yet red behind the hills, lights
the iron bed you partly see, and you know
above the quilt, on the wall you cannot see,
the photograph of the lanky man
in cap and wrinkled clothes
still hangs. She would not have moved it.

Mornings you came before dawn to her house,
sent by your daddy, wood-basket full in your arms.
Tailings of coal lined the floor,
the dingy helmet lamp hung behind the door.
You long remembered the shade of his good shirt,
spread of the hands that stoked the church stove
Sundays before your father walked next door.
And then that midnight
awakened by neighbors, you hung
on your father's coat through blowing
snow, sat with her, cold by the door,
watched the table lamp's wild flickering
over a few hand-lettered sheets: *Union.*

His truck found off Raton Pass,
friends carried his body up with ropes, buried
him behind the house, deep
in January as they could dig.

In time, his presence grew dimmer, taller.
Daily you learned the weight
of wood, the taste of her cookies, nearly sweet,
her greying hair and her silences endless as snow,
your boy voice reading from the book in your hands –
how your voice trailed from the last page
as the stove crackled and wind scoured the door.
Three days after you turned eighteen,
you boarded the train for Denver. She
stood on the platform, smoke
billowing over her, and wrapped
his old scarf around your neck.

Here in this town, where children still
turn eighteen and leave, someone rings
the church bell. Forgive me. It rings
familiar in the growing dark, echoes
through the empty houses and abandoned
lives. From this far wall, the house
seems larger. Beyond the open door, the sun
setting behind the blue hills, casts loose its light
across the floor, the iron stove,
the table, the lamp, the chairs.

Wind ravels leaves across the yard,
blows the gate against the fence
with a dry rattle. The porch swing creaks,
beats at the house. It's 1940.
Father, you're twenty,
come back to a house you remembered differently.
Still, down the road through bare trees,
there's the one street light, and beyond, the midnight
blue of town: that corner where your father died suddenly
last Christmas on the post office steps,
the lighted window above the dry goods store
where Mr. Meyers still rocks, victim
of the war. He searched the town for you
years ago when your mother's quiet death
sent you hiding under the bed.
His deep cough shook the house gone silent,
rabbled in your ear.

Your sisters tried to keep the vines
from taking over, shutters from falling,
sold furniture a little at a time.
Inside, the birthday cake is covered
with a dishcloth; Father's felt hat
is stiff on the closet shelf.
Madge must, as always,
take your picture as you hold the cake.
Later, you'll lie in your cold room and listen
to the swing hitting the house, the night
train passing under the bridge,
its distant, longing whistle,
and imagine the house sold when Ruby marries,
when Madge needs money.
Years later, she'll send you photographs
of what you don't or won't say you remember:
house, birthday cake, the funeral you dressed darkly for,
and this one beside the train billowing black.
You've cocked your patient half-grin. The wind
whips your overcoat, the handkerchiefs they'll wave
as you leave town.

PLAZA DE MAYO

October's air is azure
as the blossoms of the jacaranda trees
where, a usual Thursday
in Buenos Aires,
the grandmothers sail
under their white headscarves,
on each a blue-stitched name.
By the compasses of their hands
they walk the circle
they have walked twenty years.

In walking so long
the grandmothers have become
the turning world –
their shoes slap rhythmic as waves;
they set islands in memory's far sea.

And above the turning world
the jacarandas,
having stood in the plaza
all their tree lives, once felt
tanks on the streets, planes
shaking the sky, let fly
their little blue papers
on which the names appear
and swirl through the city
into open windows,
onto magnificient fountains,
out to sea,
settling upon the day's mail,
the whale-coloured water,
or the hair of a woman
who does not yet know
her first, true name.

EMALINE

Thirty-four miles north of Chinook it hangs
on the only curve of earth as always, as though
to collapse into the fenceless void
between this ground and Saskatchewan
would be relief. The house
I wanted for years to burn with him in it,
where under the ironing board of his penis
I ground my teeth and grew.
He pressed me like wind.
And wind it was Mother sacrificed me for
and meat and a cut-down coat,
the predictabilities of weather and men.
I turn the car into the yard.
That crazy tree still alive, a failure
as shelter, threatens even now
to bulge green, risk another spring
unpruned, thick with winterkill
and reflected, as though admired, by the window
behind which Mother waits on her need of me.

This is how you kill a chicken:
first, catch the chicken.
Grab it by the feet with one hand. Wrap
your arm around its wings to keep it
from beating you to death. Take the head
with your other hand and let go
of the feet. Swing it over your head
until you hear it pop and crack.
This is what I did Sundays
(we never went to church)
but he wanted the dinner.

This is how the cat
would take young pheasants
from their nests: take them
by the neck in his teeth and shake
until the bird lay limp in the mouth,
thus feeding the predator's hunger.

Scarred ground where the outhouse stood
until it collapsed on its own, assisted by wind,
where he'd follow me, the thing
ascending in his pants and down my throat
until I hardly could go without vomit
coiling up within me.
There were nights she pretended to sleep
while he pretended to tuck me in.
My premenstural blood spotted the sheets,
sheets washed weekly in concern
for cleanliness, blood unremarkable.
Sure, I'll move her out if she wants,
drive her to the rest home in Chinook.
That's easy as his funeral was easy,
as the first and final clods of dirt dropped
from my hands, the old, dried *no's*
that hit with discernable force.

No I never said for myself
but for my brown-skinned daughters
he never spoke to. I brought them here
only when my marriage failed,
when this house was safer than my own.
Mother blamed his skin but I,
having never known love's daily gestures,
settled for need. It was a hot night, how
in summer wind lay fallow
just when you wanted it.
We set the radio in the window, danced
until dark, me and the kids and some chickens,
and always one of us swinging little Rachael
on our hips. That night
I leaned a chair against the door
of our room and when the knob
began to move, I said it.
No.
The knob stopped and my no
echoed through twenty years of fear.

I shivered through that night
as my children sweated and slept.
At four I rose in the colourless room
and packed our things, not knowing where
we would go, thinking we might head north
(it was easier in those days),
and loaded the car. And coming back to the house
I looked up at last to see
that our tree, thick with winterkill was green,
deep green and showered in its own leaves
below the incurious clouds,
before the dim audacity of the dawn.

Petulant hawk,
swinging that high pine
like the angel thrust by unmerciful hands
onto the Christmas tree,
this winter sky is sewn up
like a mouth full of secrets.
No matter – I'm speaking to you.
Once heavy with them,
now I bear the weight of my son
who clings by legs and arms
to my waist and neck
and I am no longer laden with secrets.
That girl following us – head down,
notebook of poems clutched to her chest –
you flew at her, swept claw and wing
about her face until she shuffled along, hunched.
Bird of Mother's madness,
you ate lies Mommy tossed about her past:
the friendly father, midwest bliss.
You ripped at the meat of childhood.
Mommy's rage threw open
your wings, your perch
the nest of her hair.

The path widens; leaves lie
like wings, feathers frozen underfoot.
I was the girl, beautiful to no one,
who learned to hide the binder
of dangerous words in ever
original places,
while Mommy flew through the room
for it, ripped pages
that fed her paranoia,
suspected me of knowing her truth.
I'd tuck it into the atlas,
zip it into my pillow. You thumped
the glass, shifted eyes at my windowsill.
In time, I hid those memories even from myself,
until I began to trip over them, unexpected,
while pulling up a grocery list,
shaking out clean sheets in the night
for a sick child.

Now the loosened latch, the gate
marking a clean circumference
in the dirt, now the horses'
warm fog of breath. Hawk,
I survived you. Vane of wind,
of storm, I still fashion
poems to raise like kites
into the ebullient air, mouths
to spill open the sky, tongues
for speech.

HOW ABUELITA REELED ME IN

for Claudia Victoria Poblete
and her grandmother

My life has been framed
by bars. Beginning and end.
                    Buenos Aires, 1978.
Now, 21 years later. And in between,
the net of bars that crashed across the elevator door
in the apartment building of my father,
                              the General.
Smiling, he showed the bars of his teeth –
narrow, separated. So many years
I didn't know. Didn't know who he was;
didn't know who I was.

My baby picture sat on a lace cloth on the table,
where, daily, the mail was tossed. Beside the table
our small TV. Beside the TV a window. In summers,
window open, we wilted on the 4th floor
and taxis clogging the street below
                    sounded like rain.
Winters, window shut, the rain in the streets
sounded like rain.

One day in the TV a woman, shouting
in a crowd of women, wore around her neck
                    the same photo of me
that sat on our table. I said, "Papá, why
is that woman wearing my photo?" And my father
the General, who never spoke about where he had been
in his days or his nights, stared. He clicked
                    his obedient heels
and turned. "She is a witch, and she wants
to steal your blood." I didn't know
then, at 16, how my life had begun,
about the bars of my babyhood.

Because I could not yet walk, my mother
carried me into the jail the night they came for her.
Before my General father ordered her death,
                    he carried me home
to the apartment of continuous rain. My new mother
smoked and took long café lunches.

So many years passed, and on a day that tasted like soap
the new government came for the General.
                    The women from TV
clotted the street and shouted.
"Don't let the witch steal your blood,"
were his final words to me.

Then one day I swam the *subte*
to the city centre, walked a dozen blocks
and crossed the raging Avenida 9 de Julio
where I sat in a café and took coffee
for an hour, eyeing the offices across the street.
At last, I felt my body rise and go
toward the DNA clinic for children
                    of the disappeared.

Months later, they called me
and we met, my grandmother and I,
each holding our photos. It was then
I learned my name and my mother's
and my father's names. I learned of their deaths
and my life of bars. In front of the door
to my grandmother's apartment
is an iron gate, but the gate
                    sits open.
Rusted from decades of rain, her gate
cannot be shut.

THE VIEW

This is the time of which it is written:
"You will be asked how you spent all the time
that has been given to you."
— The Cloud of Unknowing

I.
I'd had no idea my view
had foreshortened so — the beautiful
wiped clear away. It happened
gradually, with the incident
over the rattlesnake, a skunk
in the basement. Then that whole
long winter, spring cracking
the brutal snow. For weeks thereafter
I shuddered, wakened nights — a cougar
was prowling close to the house, and I,
so often alone with two small children. Evidence
lay just behind the pitiful garden —
a doe, stretched out in the grass,
hindquarters stripped clean
down to bone.

They say that's exactly and all a cougar
will eat of a deer, that what is sensible
to one creature appears senseless
to another. Cecilia learned it on that ranch,
absolute middle of Montana, when
she caught a view of the half-eaten doe
from atop her father's shoulders. The sight
disturbed her sleep, and in those weeks
one of us had to lie with her in order
to soothe her wakings. How the baby
grew and opened his hands, how
the trees relaxed their shocking green fists,
I can't now remember.

II.
June, rainy and dark.
I stood at the kitchen window
and tracked the swelling river, wiped
highchairs and faces of mis-targeted food,
imagined rattlers in the field
and thought of the cougar
like a robber, still at large.
Wrung my hands like dishcloths
at the sink.

One evening after dinner,
my husband strapped each of us into the car
and drove the narrow shelf of road
along the hill behind our place. Carefully
he manouvered the hardening ruts,
hugged the hill's cliff face
as we rocked inside the womb of the car
and our house grew small. Rounding the hill,
I watched the sun dissolve and part
the clouds. My kitchen window river
shimmered and spilled into the great
Missouri. Cattle grazed the green hill.
New calves had been born
since last I had thought of cows,
their faces white, eyes wide as a child's.
And beyond in the lucent evening lay
cliffs of the *pishkun,* buffalo jump,
bright flat buttes rising far
from my usual view, the distant
snow-peaked mountains.

ACKNOWLEDGMENTS

Acknowledgment is gratefully made to the following periodicals in which poems from this book were first published:

Anglican Theological Review: "Annunciation Street"
Borderlands: Texas Poetry Review: "Perpetuity"
Carolina Quarterly: "Album: Altered Figures"
Commonweal: "The Letters"
CutBank: "Santa Elena Crossing"
Descant: "How Abuelita Reeled Me In"
Equinox: "The Fabric of Mercy"
Image: Seattle Arts Commission: "The Locked House"
    (under the title, "The Living")
Iowa Woman: "Vigil"
North American Review: "Cecilia's Face"
Other Side: "Mothers," "A Medicine for the Living"
Phoebe: "Witnesses"
Quarterly West: "Final Reunion"
Seattle Review: "The Railroad Watch"
Sojourners: "Montana, Early Spring"
    (under the title, "Early Spring in a Dark Time")
Sunrust: "Bearers of Darkness"
Visions International: "Emaline"

"Plaza de Mayo" and "Montana, Early Spring" (under the title, "Early Spring in a Dark Time") appeared in *Poems for the Luminous World,* Frog Hollow Press, 2002.

"Benediction" won 2nd prize in Glimmer Train Press's April 2003 Poetry Open.

An earlier version of this manuscript was semi-finalist for the Kenyon Review Prize, the Winnow Press First Book Award, the Kore Press First Book competition, and was finalist for the Autumn House Press open competition and the White Pine Press Book Award.

My thanks to John Skoyles who encouraged me long ago and to Russell Thorburn, both of whom read and commented on versions of this work; to The Waywords – Andrea, Barbara, Cynthia, Grace, Karen, and Yvonne, tough critics all; to Wendy Morton, queen of Mocambopo; and to Lorna Crozier and Patrick Lane, mentors to many.

ABOUT THE AUTHOR

Pamela Porter is an award-winning poet and juvenile fiction author. Her poetry has been published in periodicals across Canada and the United States and beyond, from *Grain, Descant,* and *Arc,* to the *Atlanta Review, North American Review,* and *Storie* from Rome, Italy. She has twice been a finalist in the CBC/*Saturday Night* Canadian Literary Awards and has been on the shortlist for the Pushcart Prize, the *Atlanta Review* International Poetry Contest, and the National Poetry Series manuscript competition in Princeton, New Jersey. *Stones Call Out* is her first poetry book publication. Her free-verse children's book *The Crazy Man* received the 2005 Governor General's Award for Children's Literature.

Born in Albuquerque, Pamela Porter has also lived in Texas, Louisiana, Washington, and Montana. She obtained her undergraduate English degree from Southern Methodist University in Dallas, and received her MFA in Creative Writing from the University of Montana. She currently lives in Sidney, BC.